What can I ...?

Hear

Sue Barraclough

Little Nippers

www.heinemann.co.uk/library
Visit our website to find out more information about **Heinemann Library** books.

To order:
☎ Phone 44 (0) 1865 888066
📄 Send a fax to 44 (0) 1865 314091
💻 Visit the Heinemann Bookshop at www.heinemann.co.uk/library to browse our catalogue and order online.

First published in Great Britain by Heinemann Library, Halley Court, Jordan Hill, Oxford OX2 8EJ, part of Harcourt Education. Heinemann is a registered trademark of Harcourt Education Ltd.

Editorial: Sarah Shannon and Louise Galpine
Design: Jo Hinton-Malivoire and Tokay,
   Bicester, UK (www.tokay.co.uk)
Picture Research: Melissa Allison
Production: Camilla Smith

Originated by Chroma Graphics (Overseas) Pte.Ltd.
Printed and bound in China by South China Printing Company

ISBN 0 431 02203 8 (hardback)
09 08 07 06 05
10 9 8 7 6 5 4 3 2 1

ISBN 0 431 02209 7 (paperback)
09 08 07 06 05
10 9 8 7 6 5 4 3 2 1

British Library Cataloguing in Publication Data
Barraclough, Sue
What can I? – Hear
612.8'5
A full catalogue record for this book is available from the British Library.

Acknowledgements
The Publishers would like to thank the following for permission to reproduce photographs:
Alamy p.**9**; Bubbles p.**18** (Richard Yard); Corbis p.**5** top; Corbis SABA pp.**16-17** (Louise Gubb); DK Images p.**15** bottom; Getty Images / PhotoDisc pp.**12-13**, **19** bottom; Getty Images / Stone p.**14**; Harcourt Education pp.**10-11** (Gareth Boden), **8** (Trevor Clifford), **4**, **6-7**, **22-23** (Tudor Photography), p.**5** right (Pete Morris); Nature Photo Library p.**5** left (Doug Weschler); NHPA p.**19** top and right (Ernie Janes); Quadrant Picture Library p.**15** top; Robert Harding Picture Library p.**15** right; Superstock pp. **20-21**.

Cover photograph reproduced with permission of Harcourt Education Ltd. / Gareth Boden.

Every effort has been made to contact copyright holders of any material reproduced in this book. Any omissions will be rectified in subsequent printings if notice is given to the Publishers.

Contents

What **sounds** wake you up in the morning?

Breakfast sounds

Brrring!
Brrring!

The telephone is **ringing!**

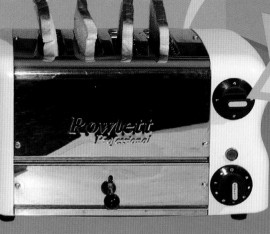

Is your house **noisy** or **quiet** in the morning?

Pop!

Loud and quiet

Twang!

Bang!

Boom!

Rattle!

Toys make loud noises.

Purr, purr.

When it is quiet you can hear soft sounds.

Splish, splash!

Splas...

Whoosh!

Gurgle!

There are lots of **noises** you can make with water.

10

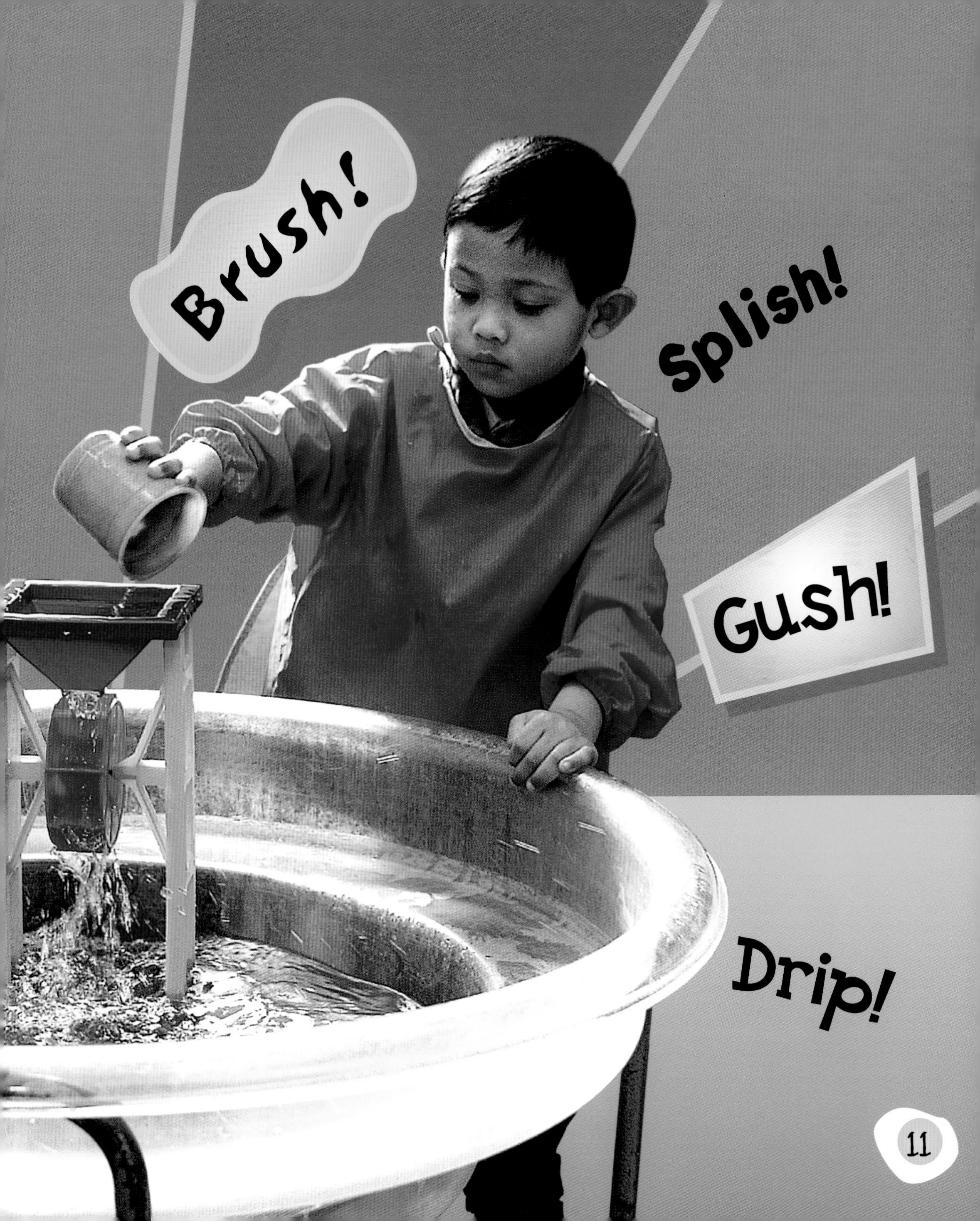
Brush!
Splish!
Gush!
Drip!

Pitter, patter

Rain can be noisy. **Pitter**, patter, drip, **drop**, splish, splash!

Rumble, rumble!

Can you think of other weather noises?

Crunch, crunch!

Traffic noise

Look and **listen** for traffic
as you cross the road.

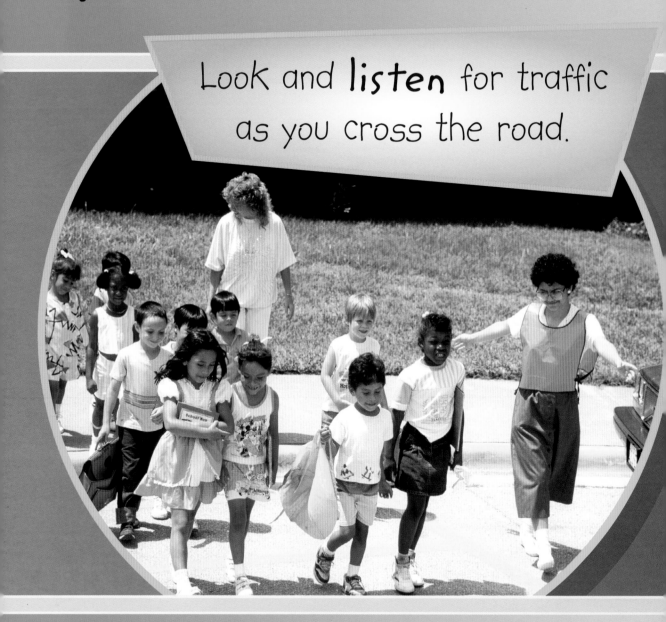

What is the **loudest** traffic sound?

Honk, honk!

Vroom, vroom!

Ding, ding!

Can you make a **noise** like a train?

17

Animal noises

Baaaa!

Glug, glug!

Animals make lots of different sounds!

What is your favourite animal **sound**?

Chirp, chirp

Oink, oink!

oooo!

Birds and bees

Tweet

Tweet!

If you listen carefully you will hear sounds all around us.

What sounds can you hear now?

bzzzzzz!

Bedtime sounds

shhh!

Goodnight!

Index

Notes for adults

This series encourages children to explore their environment to gain knowledge and understanding of the things they can see, smell, hear, taste, and feel. The following Early Learning Goals are relevant to the series:

• use the senses to explore and learn about the world around them
• respond to experiences and describe, express, and communicate ideas
• make connections between new information and what they already know
• ask questions about why things happen and how things work
• discover their local environment and talk about likes and dislikes.

The following additional information may be of interest
The ear acts like a funnel to take sound waves into the inner ear. The inner parts of the ear pick up these vibrations and turn them into nerve signals that are passed on to the brain.

Follow-up activities
Develop ideas and understanding by encouraging children to notice how they respond to different sounds, and identifying different sounds around them. Use music and sounds as stimulus for imaginative play. Make simple instruments such as shakers or drums to explore different sounds.